THE MASTERS 3 | *Canaletto*

KNOWLEDGE PUBLICATIONS

Canaletto

KEITH ROBERTS

ADVISORY EDITOR

Canaletto 1697-1768

Giovanni Antonio Canal, known as Canaletto, was born in Venice on October 18th, 1697. His father, Bernardo Canal, was a painter and designer of theatrical scenery and the young Canaletto was trained in the family workshop. In the years 1716-18 he was working with his father and his brother, Cristoforo, at the Teatro S. Angelo and the Teatro S. Cassiano in Venice. In 1719-20, all three were in Rome, where they painted the scenery for productions of Scarlatti's operas Tito Sempronio Gracco and Turno Aricino. Canaletto was back in Venice in 1720, the year in which his name first appears in the fraglia (roster) of Venetian painters.

About this time, Canaletto decided that the theatre was not going to offer sufficient scope for his talents. He wanted to be a fully fledged landscape painter. Having made up his mind to change course, he quickly realised that he could make a great deal of money, of which he is known to have been very fond, with pictures of the scenery and customs of his native Venice, as great a tourist centre then as it is today.

Unfortunately, very little is known about the extra training he must have undergone. But it is likely that he paid close attention to the careful, topographical views, primarily of Rome and Venice, painted by expatriate Northern artists like Gaspar Van Wittel (1653-1736). And he certainly studied the rather stodgy paintings of Venetian landmarks and ceremonies that were being produced on the spot by Luca Carlevaris (1663-1730).

Canaletto's rise to fame was swift. By March, 1722, he was already in touch with the kind of wealthy Englishmen (often visitors to Venice) who were always to remain his best clients. By 1727 he was so busy he could afford to turn down commissions and by 1736 his prices were five times what they had been only ten years before. The English connection was strengthened by an association, no doubt to mutual advantage, with Joseph Smith, an English merchant, publisher and art collector who became British Consul in Venice in 1740. Smith not only commissioned pictures to keep (there were over fifty Canalettos in his collection when it was bought by George III in 1762) but must also have acted as an agent as well. And he helped to spread the artist's fame even wider with the prints he published (1735 and 1742).

Canaletto was able to satisfy the large demand for his work because he employed assistants. These are known to have included his nephew, Bernardo Bellotto (1720-80), who went on to achieve independent fame in Saxony, Austria and Poland.

So efficient did Canaletto become that he was able to cope with orders in bulk. In the second half of the 1730s, the 4th Earl of Carlisle bought over a dozen canvases, of which Plate IV is one.

In 1741 came the outbreak of the War of the Austrian Succession. Actually or potentially, the conflict involved most of Europe. Foreign touring became hazardous and the number of visitors to Venice dwindled rapidly. With his acute eye for business, Canaletto began to develop alternative commodities, suitable for the home market: etchings, fanciful views, Roman scenes and pictures of non-tourist centres like Padua and Brenta.

The war continued and the stratagem did not prove, perhaps, as successful as Canaletto had hoped. In May, 1746, he came to England with a letter of introduction to the Duke of Richmond. Save for two return visits to Venice (autumn, 1750 and summer, 1753) he remained in Britain until about 1755. The views that he produced were of country houses and places of interest in and around London.

Canaletto returned to Venice in about 1755. He continued to run a studio (Guardi may have studied with him for a time) and he produced elaborate, finished drawings, but both the volume and the quality of his painting declined. This may have been partly due to ill health. Having twice failed to gain admission to the Venetian Academy (landscape was considered an inferior branch of art in the 18th century), Canaletto was finally elected in 1763. He died of fever, in Venice, on April 20th, 1768. For a long time after his death, until the advent of photography in fact, fakes and pastiches of Canaletto's work continued to appear on the market.

'His excellency lies in painting things which fall immediately under his eye'

These words were written in a letter written from Venice on November 28th, 1727 by Owen McSwiney to the Duke of Richmond.

One of the most important ways in which the creative artist differs from the rest of us is in his ability to see in objects, if he is a painter or if he is a writer, in situations and people, more than meets the eye. It is a form of intuition that enables the artist to sense the skull beneath the skin; the character behind the remark; the underlying pattern. Blessed with this gift, he can, in his own work, imply character in lines of dialogue or, if he is painting a landscape, not only give us the visual facts but also, in the very way he presents them, suggest the spirit in which the finished picture should be studied. Claude, for example, painted trees, hills, water and fields quite accurately but he arranged his details in such a way that his main *idea*, a dream of a Golden Age when man lived in perfect harmony with nature, is absolutely clear. He stamped the scene with his own point of view.

Not all artists have this ability to invest an object in a painting or a character in a play with ideas. Sometimes it is because they do not have the technique, they are not clever enough, and sometimes it is because they do not have any ideas in the first place. Canaletto comes within the second category. He did not wish to suggest that Nature was essentially brutal, or that it was primarily a manifestation of God's sublime handiwork. He painted straightforward views.

The lack of ideas in Canaletto's work constitutes a definite weakness and it is one of several reasons why he can never be called a great artist. And yet it is this very deficiency that has helped to save him from neglect. The disadvantage of works of art that embody ideas and philosophies, however noble and sublime, is that they are at the mercy of changes in the intellectual climate. Philosophies fall into disrepute. Ideas revered by one generation seem absurd to the next. English Victorian painting is hard to come to terms with nowadays because its sentimentality and moral fervour are alien to mid-20th century thinking.

Canaletto's pictures are not profound but they exert a spell far stronger than many works of greater significance because the basis of their appeal has remained so fundamentally unchanged. Views of Venice designed to give nothing but pleasure are as much in demand as they ever were.

Canaletto's pictures have other qualities denied to deeper and graver spirits. They are, for one thing, enormous fun. Having no biases, no philosophic or theoretic reasons for singling out one object in preference to another, Canaletto could dwell on everything with dispassionate curiosity. Chimney pots, shutters, brickwork, rigging, pie-sellers, wigs, there was nothing too humble or too trivial for his attention. His pictures can be studied in the same spirit as one reads a gossip column; and, what is more, a gossip column tinged with poetry. For Canaletto could not help but stress the unique character of Venice herself. The shimmering alliance of stone and water gives to every detail and every incident a charm and fascination they would surely lack had the artist chosen to incorporate them in views of Pittsburg or Stoke-on-Trent.

It is important to note that Canaletto had no great philosophic ideas about landscape. But it does not follow that the introduction of a little 18th-century philosophy at the time would have been enough to consign his work to the lumber rooms now. The views in this album may be intellectually and spiritually limited but they have never ceased to be visually positive. Canaletto's skill was prodigious and he had an unfailing flair for composition. He knew exactly how to organise a vast quantity of detail without making the picture look fussy or overloaded.

IN ANY discussion of his work, it is important to stress Canaletto's origins. From his childhood days he assisted his father and brother in the family trade of scene painting and it was not until he was at least twenty that he began to think of specialising in landscape painting. His youth was thus passed under the dominating influence of the paternal workshop. This training left Canaletto with certain im-

3

pressions that, it is no exaggeration to say, shaped his entire career. These impressions were of two kinds, the one practical, the other stylistic.

The art of designing and painting scenery was—and, indeed, still is—a practical art. The scale and speed with which it was produced demanded collaboration; changes at rehearsal stage might necessitate alteration; while public reaction had to be constantly borne in mind. The successful scene painter had to be flexible, adaptable and willing to collaborate. There was no place here for the visionary artist, who worked alone, as the spirit moved him.

MOST 18th-century artists, it is true, were prepared to see their art in terms of merchandise, with a corresponding acceptance of current taste and public demand, but few were quite as business-like as Canaletto. He pushed up his prices in the 1720s and 1730s quite ruthlessly and throughout his life he employed any number of assistants. He naturally painted works to order and he did not tire of producing as many as a dozen versions of the same view (the case with Plate X). And when the English customers stayed away from Venice, on account of the War of the Austrian Succession, he followed them to England. It is hard to believe that Canaletto would have been quite so practical if he had not been brought up in quite so practical an environment. And it is difficult to imagine that he would have taken such a dispassionate and prosaic view of his own work had he not been trained in a profession where the prime significance of the product was its utility.

Canaletto's early training also affected his style, influencing the way he constructed his paintings. The kind of stage scenery fashionable in north Italy when he was a youth consisted of elaborate architecture, with colonnades and porticos, seen in sharp perspective, and with the vanishing point to right or left of centre. The final impression tended to be of a single, uninterrupted vista. This is one of the chief characteristics of Canaletto's painted views. In the *Grand Canal Looking towards Santa Maria della Salute* (Plate X) or the *Venice: Square and Church of the Gesuiti* (Plate XI) the lines converge on a single vanishing point. Even when this is out of the picture, as it is in *The Piazza of San Marco* (Plate IV), the eye is caught up in the web of narrowing lines as they move across the picture.

When the paintings are not vistas, they are panoramas, such as the magnificent *Bucintoro returning to the Molo on Ascension Day* (Plate VI and VII) or the *Venice: The Feast Day of St. Roch* (Plate IX). In both types of view Canaletto stresses the basic character. In the vistas the vanishing point is emphasised. While the panoramas are elaborately casual in construction, as impersonally all-embracing as the view through a movable telescope.

Common to both, is the absence of serious interruptions in the foreground or middle distance. In the landscapes of Claude, Poussin or Constable, there are often trees in the front, masking sections of the distance. By means of this device, which creates contrasts in scale, painters were able to increase the sense of space within the picture. In the theatre, this sense of space would have been achieved by the human actors moving in front of the scenery and by extra strips of scenery at the sides. It was enough that the actual backdrop be a single, uninterrupted vista or panorama. Although he changed his style, Canaletto's pictures always retained the closest links with the traditions of the theatrical backdrop. And this is perhaps why, crowded and lively though the canvases are, one always feels at such a distance from the scene. Canaletto's paintings never induce any feelings of intimate contact with nature.

It has been stated that Canaletto was business-like and his case is an unusually clear example of the way financial ambition can affect an artist's career.

Canaletto's early works (Plates I to III) are very carefully painted. The brushwork is lively and great care is taken with details, such as the shipping in Plate II or the house on the left in *The Stonemason's Yard* (Plate III). *The Stonemason's Yard* is, in fact, Canaletto's masterpiece. In this, as in no other painting, he combines prodigious technical skill with the desire to give every single object, whether it be the stones that litter the shadowed yard, or

2. *THE TOWER OF MALGHERA.* MUSEO CORRER, VENICE

4

3. PORTICO WITH A LANTERN. MUSEO CORRER, VENICE

the high balcony on the right with the precariously balanced flower pots, a sense of its own individuality. Canaletto makes us feel that he cared for such humble things. The picture has, in addition to its skill, a quality that can only be described as touching.

Everything about these early views is weighty and considered. The figures are thought out individually and were probably based on sketches. The colouring of the skies is carefully graded and the shadows treated with care. Even the texture of walls is presented in lively detail. But although Canaletto may have been satisfied with the quality of his pictures, we may deduce that one thing seriously worried him. They were taking too long to paint. Determined to make money, and in large quantities, he was soon concerned not with improving the quality of his art but with stepping up the quantity of his merchandise.

The Stonemason's Yard does not represent the popular view of Venice and, like the four pictures painted in 1725-6 for Stefano Conti of Lucca, it was probably produced for a local patron, who would have found the unfamiliar aspects of the city more interesting than the celebrated sights with which he would have been all too familiar. But Canaletto knew that the best customers were foreigners, and in particular the wealthy Englishmen making the Grand Tour of Europe. Cutting his coat according to the cloth, he began to concentrate on popular views.

But the most important issue was still the time factor. What he had to do was to abbreviate his technique, find shortcuts, and evolve a style in which any number of assistants could participate without the unity of the finished product being impaired. How he went about this process of mechanisation can be studied in the plates reproduced in this album.

The Grand Canal (Plate II) is a very early work, dateable about 1723, and as in *The Stonemason's Yard* the different phenomena are treated with a marked feeling for their individual qualities and visual flavour. The water has the rippling, silky sheen of real water. The loaded boats lie heavy on the canal. And the group of people squatting on the grass does not seem to be contrived but rather an inevitable part of the city. Plate X represents the same view painted seven to ten years later. The character is subtly different. The water is now shown as an endless series of curly strokes, like unravelled wool. There is far less sense of detail. The figures on the bank not only look like afterthoughts; they actually were painted later. The lines of the pavement can be seen through the man standing in front of the barrel.

Canaletto learned how to reduce all the elements in the picture to the status of a formula and this naturally affected the character of the painting. *The Piazza of San Marco* (Plate IV), for example, is less subtly painted than *The Stonemason's Yard* but its impact is sharper and it is more obviously entertaining. This is partly because of the colour, which is (like all Canaletto's colouring after about 1730) brighter, harder and clearer. As with the concentration on popular views, this change of tone may have been dictated by the higher selling potentiality of the brighter kind of image.

ALWAYS anxious to make studio procedures efficient, Canaletto came to rely on a portable form of *camera obscura*. This is a relatively simple device—a series of adjustable lenses and mirrors contained within a box—that projects on to a piece of paper (or a canvas or screen) a panorama of the scene in front of the lens. Although Canaletto must have learned a good deal about perspective in the family workshop, his early pictures are not always very convincing. Looking at Plates I and II, one has the feeling that the ground level is on the slope and that the figures and boats are in danger of sliding to the bottom of the canvas. Plate IV was painted in the 1730s and it shows the degree of mastery Canaletto was able to reach with the help of the *camera obscura*.

The mechanisation of Canaletto's style was never, fortunately, total, and it did not, of course, take place all at once. *Venice: The Feast Day of St. Roch* (Plate IX: c. 1735) shows the painter responding with much of his original, ebullient feeling for what is distinct and individual.

The spectacular *Bucintoro returning to the Molo on Ascension Day* (Plates VI and VII), produced about 1730, re-

4. PADUA: THE
PORTELLO AND
THE BRENTA
CANAL.
WINDSOR CASTLE
Reproduced by
gracious per-
mission of Her
Majesty the
Queen.

veals both processes in operation at the same time. The foreground figures, and in particular the group on the left with the gondolas in collision, are vivid and fresh. They communicate a sense of direct observation. On the other hand, the water, the distant crowds and the ornate barges are reduced to the level of mannered calligraphy.

In his main aims, Canaletto succeeded. He became a great success and he was able to sustain a large output. He could satisfy bulk orders (such as the 22 companion views now at Woburn Abbey (Plates V and XII), and repeat designs with unwearying competence. Canaletto was at the height of his fame from the late 1720s to the mid-1740s; but even in these years there were hints that all was not well. In 1739 the French writer, Des Brosses, remarked that 'the English have completely spoiled him by offering three times as much as he asks' for his work.

In 1745, Canaletto travelled to England to bolster up his business, which had been seriously undermined by the outbreak of war. He came with letters of introduction to the Duke of Richmond, for whom he immediately painted two views of London. Still family property, these pictures are in many ways the best of the English views. The artist was no doubt anxious to make a good impression in a new country.

Canaletto did not, however, maintain the renewed promise of these two canvases. Soon rumours were circulating that he was not the 'veritable Canaletto of Venice' at all. Much of this was no doubt malicious gossip engendered in the art trade, but the weakness of the English pictures must have had a lot to do with it. Especially as so many of the finer earlier paintings of Venice were readily available in Britain for comparison. To counteract the scurrilous rumours, Canaletto twice (in 1749 and again in 1751) put advertisements in the papers announcing public exhibitions of new and elaborate specimens of his art.

The basis for complaint can be studied here in Plates XIV and XVI. In comparison with the early works, the drawing is certainly very slick and the tendency to see figures as connected blobs of colour (and this is, incidentally, what the *camera obscura* does to figures that pass its lens) has hardened into a mannerism.

To add to Canaletto's difficulties in England, there were aspects of visual life for which his almost exclusive concentration on Venice would not have prepared him. He was at first puzzled, and in the end defeated, by English gothic architecture and trees. But in spite of the grave defects, the English paintings (as well as the later Venetian canvases) are saved by Canaletto's indestructible sense of design. He gave up much but he never lost the ability to manipulate large quantities of detail. The melodies may have grown thin and repetitive but the feeling for rhythm remained.

THE LAST fifteen years of Canaletto's life were clouded. He returned to Venice about 1755 but he did not resume work on anything like the same scale. Whether this was due to ill health, disinterest or disappointment born of the not entirely satisfactory visit to England, lack of evidence makes it impossible to say. There is certainly a loss of bite in the later works. The mannerisms were confirmed and although there is a memorable account of English visitors coming across him sketching in the Piazza of S. Marco, he would seem to have preferred wholly studio work. The scenes that he produced were more and more artificial; inventions that required no recourse to direct observation of nature.

In 1763, Canaletto was finally elected to the Venetian Academy. His official 'reception picture' was the *Portico of a Palace* (dated 1765. Now in the Accademia, Venice). It is an airy and fantastic scene. Balustrades, columns, arches and stairs form a vista seen in steep perspective. The result is curiously close to the kind of scenery Canaletto must have worked on as a youth. It is almost as if he were celebrating this final honour with an ironic reference to the career he had deserted in his search for success. For by the time he gained the twice-denied place in the Academy, fame and success were beginning to ebb away.

6

The Plates

I THE PIAZZA OF SAN MARCO
Oil on canvas: 56⅜ in. × 82 in.
THYSSEN COLLECTION, LUGANO: SWITZERLAND

The heavy shadows, slightly strained perspective and rich handling of paint, are typical of Canaletto's very early work. Likely to have been painted in or before 1723 when the present marble pavement, visible in Plate IV but not here, was laid. Painted as a companion picture to Plate II.

II THE GRAND CANAL LOOKING TOWARDS SANTA MARIA DELLA SALUTE
Oil on canvas: 56⅜ in. × 82 in.
THYSSEN COLLECTION, LUGANO: SWITZERLAND

A companion to Plate I and therefore painted in or before 1723. The very strong sense of the scene as a vista links the painting to the traditions of theatrical scenery, on which Canaletto worked as a youth. Plate X is a later treatment of the same view.

III THE STONEMASON'S YARD
Oil on canvas: 48¾ in. × 64⅛ in.
NATIONAL GALLERY: LONDON

Canaletto's masterpiece, probably painted in the second half of the 1720s. The view is from the Campo St. Vidal across the Grand Canal to S. Maria della Carita, which, with the adjoining 'scuola', was suppressed in 1807. The buildings became the Accademia of Fine Arts. The picture was successfully cleaned in 1955.

IV THE PIAZZA OF SAN MARCO
Oil on canvas: 45 in. × 60½ in.
NATIONAL GALLERY OF ART: WASHINGTON

A fine example of Canaletto's second manner, with its sharper drawing, bright, clear colour and assured, even rigid, perspective. Dateable to the second half of the 1730s. One of an important group of his pictures acquired by (probably) the fourth Earl of Carlisle for his Yorkshire home, Castle Howard. They were hanging in the drawing-room by April 1745.

V THE CANNAREGIO FROM THE GRAND CANAL
Oil on canvas: 18½ in. × 31½ in.
WOBURN ABBEY

One of a set of twenty-two companion views of Venice. Precisely when they were acquired is not known; though they are recorded in the 1771 Inventory of Bedford House, London. They are likely to have been painted before 1745. Plate XII is from the same set.

VI-VII THE BUCINTORO RETURNING TO THE MOLO ON ASCENSION DAY
Oil on canvas: 71⅝ in. × 102 in.
THE ALDO CRESPI COLLECTION: MILAN

Canaletto's largest known painting, produced about 1730. The Bucintoro, or state barge, was moored in front of the Doge's Palace on Ascension Day, when the annual ceremony of symbolically marrying Venice to the Adriatic took place. The Doge, with senators and other notables, would embark and be rowed to the Porto di Lido, where he would cast a gold ring into the sea.

VIII THE BASIN OF ST. MARK'S, LOOKING EAST
Oil on canvas: 49⅜ in. × 60¼ in.
MUSEUM OF FINE ARTS: BOSTON

Both this and Plate VI are good examples of Canaletto's command of the panoramic view. Dateable to the early 1730s. It must have been produced after 1726-8, when the onion-shaped steeple of San Giorgio Maggiore (right centre) was put up, and before 1745, when the non-visible church of the Pietà was begun.

IX *VENICE: THE FEAST DAY OF ST. ROCH*
Oil on canvas: 58⅛ in. × 78½ in.
NATIONAL GALLERY: LONDON

The Doge (Alvise Pisani?) is shown leaving the church of St. Roch after the annual service to celebrate the deliverance of Venice from the Plague of 1575-6. The Doge is accompanied by members of the Signoria, the Senate and the Diplomatic Corps. One of the many picturesque Venetian customs and ceremonies that attracted visitors and which Canaletto often incorporated in his work.

X *THE GRAND CANAL LOOKING TOWARDS SANTA MARIA DELLA SALUTE*
Oil on canvas: 20⅞ in. × 27½ in.
PINACOTECA DI BRERA: MILAN

The same view as in Plate II. At least twelve other versions by Canaletto himself are known. Notice how he alters the chimney pots on the right and the windows on the shadowed wall of the palace on the left. These changes were often made not because of actual alterations so much as caprice on the part of the painter.

XI *VENICE: SQUARE AND CHURCH OF THE GESUITI*
Oil on canvas: 18½ in. × 30½ in.
PRIVATE COLLECTION: MILAN

Painted c. 1730-5. One of a series of 20 Venetian views, of the same size and character, dispersed from an English private collection in about 1957. The strip of water in the distance is the Lagoon. The Gesuiti Convent, on the right, is now a barracks.

XII *THE CHURCH OF THE REDENTORE FROM THE CANAL OF THE GIUDECCA*
Oil on canvas: 18½ in. × 31½ in.
WOBURN ABBEY

From the same series as Plate V. The now demolished church of S. Giacomo is on the right. A connected drawing by Canaletto is at Windsor (Parker No. 34). Other versions of this picture are known.

XIII *A REGATTA ON THE GRAND CANAL*
Oil on canvas: 48¹⁄₁₆ in. × 72 in.
NATIONAL GALLERY: LONDON

Likely to have been painted in the late 1730s. All Canaletto's versions of this scene were based on a scheme by Luca Carlevaris, a minor artist who was important for his development as a landscape painter after he had left the theatre. The mannered treatment of detail is typical of Canaletto's mature style.

XIV-XV *ETON COLLEGE FROM ACROSS THE THAMES*
Oil on canvas: 24¼ in. × 42⅜ in.
NATIONAL GALLERY: LONDON

Many of the details in this picture are either invented or inaccurate. The church on the left never existed. The tracery of the east window of the Chapel, the crockets and the statue on the gable, and the domes on the turrets are fancies of the artist. Likely to have been painted about 1754.

XVI *WARWICK CASTLE: THE EAST FRONT FROM THE COURTYARD*
Oil on canvas: 29¼ in. × 48 in.
COLLECTION OF THE EARL OF WARWICK

One of a series of views of the Castle that were probably commissioned from Canaletto by Francis Greville, the first Earl of Warwick, who died in 1773. This picture brings out the toy-like quality that is nearly always present in Canaletto's work, and particularly in the English views.

XVII *THE ENTRANCE TO THE GRAND CANAL FROM SAN GIORGIO MAGGIORE*
Oil on canvas detail: 50 in. × 74 in.
WALLACE COLLECTION: LONDON

The view in almost exactly the opposite direction is shown in Plate VIII. Probably painted in the late 1730s. A good example of the harder, brighter and more mechanical style of the artist's maturity.

I

IX

XIII

XIV

XV